Be Humble

Navid Alipour Episode 61

If you'd asked us a year ago if we had big plans for The Rocketship Podcast, we'd probably all have told you the same thing: not particularly. It's rare to have the fortune to reflect on a significant accomplishment. It's even rarer when the achievement was (in many ways) unexpected.

In one year, thanks to the graciousness and the candor of our guests, we were able to bring the stories, lessons, advice, failures, successes, and insights of over 100 brilliant entrepreneurs to the most amazing audience of startup nuts out there. In one year, we've reached more of you than we ever could have imagined on day one. But the accomplishment isn't in the numbers.

What started out as a small side project quickly turned into something much more meaningful when we realized how impacted you were by these stories. It wasn't just about tactics and benchmarks anymore. By covering topics from customer acquisition to the emotional health of entrepreneurs, The Rocketship became just as much about the journey of entrepreneurship as it was about strategies, techniques, and applications.

Sharing this journey with you all every week has profoundly changed each of us.

We genuinely thank you for the opportunity to continue producing the podcast. It may sound trite, but it truthfully wouldn't be possible without you.

We hope you enjoy the highlights of our first year and the incredibly diverse insights from these wonderful entrepreneurs.

Cheers,

Joelle, Matt & Michael

"PEOPLE FOCUS TOO MUCH ON OUTCOME AND TOO LITTLE ON THE PROCESS OF HOW TO GET THERE."

Brian Balfour
VP GROWTH HUBSPOT

"Sell the why, not the what."

Conrad Egusa
FOUNDER PUBLICIZE

"WHEN WE PICK WHAT WE DON'T SAY, IT SAYS A LOT MORE ABOUT US THAN WHAT WE DO SAY."

Abby Covert
AUTHOR MAKE SENSE OF ANY MESS

"CAN YOU IDENTIFY A SPACE WHERE DEMAND IS UNUSUALLY HIGH, AND BE IN A UNIQUE POSITION TO FILL THAT DEMAND?"

Ian Heidt
CEO HOUSECALL

"THE ANSWER IS VERY RARELY
ONE MORE FEATURE."

Jason Cohen
FOUNDER WPENGINE

"I'M TRADING TIME FOR MONEY AND THEN
TRADING THAT MONEY FOR TIME."

SAM SOFFES
FOUNDER SOFF.ES

A LOOK INSIDE
Hiten Shah
Episode 23

by Michael Sacca

I think this is the most nervous we'd been before an interview. Despite having talked to Hiten before, we really wanted to make this a special episode. Hiten's expertise includes self-funding, outside funding, product development, marketing, and sales. He's someone we all look up to and one of the few people that have successfully built both a self-funded company, as well as a venture-backed company.

Listening to Hiten explain the difference was incredibly helpful because he broke down the differences into aspects of what drives your decision making on a daily basis. For self-funding companies, it's all about small wins and revenue. Your focus is typically on generating immediate revenue, and you're often making decisions that will affect your bottom line this week or month. You also need to be scrappy with your resources, as it takes a bit longer to build your team because you have to create the revenue streams before you hire people to maintain and grow them. For venture-backed companies, it's all about shooting for big wins and long-term strategy. Your growth goal doesn't always need to be revenue, and you're able to hire people to help you create growth rather than waiting for revenue to make your first hires.

There really is no right or wrong answer for this; it largely depends on your business model and what type of company you want to build, which requires a bit of soul searching to figure out the right model for your situation.

"The one thing I recommend everyone think about is: Are you working on the right thing, right now?" This was a big theme throughout the episode. Hiten was very clear that each experience when building a business is unique, and what worked for him may not work for you. So instead of taking his advice verbatim, he suggested continually checking in with yourself to validate if you were spending your time on the right thing, right now. This could be a multitude of things depending on your immediate goals, but staying focused and knowing exactly what you're trying to achieve is essential.

One thing to try is to routinely take a step back, be as objective as possible, and ask yourself why you're working on what you're working on. Is there something you're avoiding? Is what you're working on the most important thing you have on your plate? Is there something that would make a bigger difference for your company? Typically, if there's something we're avoiding, that could be a sign we're working on the wrong thing at the wrong time. For me, I often put off sales, cold emailing, and writing, while I typically use design and development to avoid doing those things I'm less comfortable with. It's different for everyone, but staying conscious of our weaknesses and how we spend our time as entrepreneurs is essential to our success.

The next piece of advice he laid on us changed how I thought about advertising. **"Do more value proposition advertising early on to understand and assess the demand for what you're doing."** I'd always associated advertising as a gas pedal for growth, something that you utilize when you have the rest of your sales funnel figured out and you just need more people in the top of it. Hiten suggested using advertising instead to discover what your value proposition is. If you take a few of your potential headlines you can then AB (or ABC) test them against each other before you drive traffic to your site. That way, when you spend the time to bring visitors to your site, you'll have already tested that value proposition, increasing your chances of a conversion.

So remember, taking a step back can be one of the most valuable things you do today. Stay focused, keep testing and keep your eye on the metrics that matter to your business.

"ANYTHING CATEGORIZED AS A MISTAKE IS ACTUALLY A LESSON LEARNED."

CAT NOONE
CO-FOUNDER LIBERIO

"THERE'S A PEACE THAT COMES FROM KNOWING WHERE THINGS ARE INSTEAD OF WONDERING WHAT'S BURIED IN EMAIL."

Thomas Knoll
FOUNDER PRIMELOOP

"THERE'S NOTHING MAGICAL ABOUT BUILDING A BUSINESS. IT'S SLOW, METHODICAL WORK."

Brendan Schwartz
CO-FOUNDER & CTO WISTIA

"ENGAGEMENT SHOULD BE ALL ABOUT ELEVATING YOUR COMMUNITY AND MAKING SURE THEY ACCOMPLISH THEIR GOALS."

David Sherry
FOUNDER DEATH TO THE STOCK PHOTO

"THERE'S OFTEN AN OVER-FETISHIZATION WITH TECHNOLOGY AND NOT ENOUGH FOCUS ON SOLVING REAL PROBLEMS."

Adda Birnir
CEO SKILLCRUSH

"The best hiring hack we've learned...
hire your customers."

Carolyn Kopprasch
CHIEF HAPPINESS OFFICER BUFFER

Ryan Singer

Episode 52

by Matt Goldman

Joelle and I entered into our 52nd episode feeling a bit lost with our product, Hook-Feed. We knew it was valuable, because we were using it every day and completely reliant on it. We even had customers who were using it in a similar manner and loving it. But at the same time, we were experiencing a lot of churn and knew that our positioning on our marketing site didn't match up with the benefits of using the actual product. We were selling analytics when the product really delivered value in supporting/retaining customers. It didn't take long for us to dig into this with Ryan, and the advice he shared with us resonates to this day.

We dug into the Jobs-to-Be-Done framework, and he encouraged us to stop trying to label our product.

"There's no rule that you need to describe what you're doing in one word."

He encouraged us to do the hard work of looking at our own use cases, and our best customers use cases, and displaying those front and center.

Working on a product like Basecamp for so long, which is used in countless different ways, he completely understood the challenges of knowing who to market to, as well as how to sell the value your product or service delivers.

"We tend to use categories to talk about what we're selling rather than speaking to the problem we're solving."

Step back and look at your own product. Are you selling features on your homepage — or are you telling the story of how successful potential customers will be with your app?

Are you showing them screenshots — or are you describing painful situations that they'll completely relate to?

Think about your interactions with the products you come across on a daily basis! Most aren't memorable, but every once in a while, you come across a website that just "gets it." Before you even get to the bottom of the page, your credit card is out, you're leaning towards the screen, and you're screaming, "Shut up and take my money!"

The next time you experience this, think about what they said that struck a chord with you. What were you searching for when you found their product or service? What questions did you have that needed answering? What did they say, and why was it so valuable to you at that point in time? What job were you hoping they'd solve, and how did they convince you they were the ones who were able to solve it?

This isn't an easy process, and it should be consistently applied throughout your design, development, and marketing processes. It's so easy to get off-track — Ryan reminds us to think about, and talk to, our customers to better understand them and build a product they'll use and love.

"Situations where things go wrong are opportunities to show people how you handle it and increase trust."

Colin Nederkoorn
CEO CUSTOMER.IO

"Every year there's a new class of freshmen. If you can teach them something, you'll win."

Tawheed Kader
CEO AT TOUTAPP

"Before Treehouse, I thought:
This isn't what I want to die doing.
I want to die doing something bigger."

Ryan Carson
FOUNDER TREEHOUSE

"The most important thing you can learn to do is to sell yourself."

Josh Long
CO-FOUNDER SIMPLECAST

"WE TEND TO USE CATEGORIES TO TALK ABOUT
WHAT WE'RE SELLING RATHER THAN SPEAKING TO
THE PROBLEM WE'RE SOLVING."

Ryan Singer
PRODUCT MANAGER BASECAMP

"If you want to lose 10 pounds, you don't hit the gym twice and expect results. Same goes for blogging."

Mark Roberge
CHIEF REVENUE OFFICER HUBSPOT

A LOOK INSIDE
Adii Pienaar
Episode 9

by Michael Sacca

When we talked to Adii Pienaar, he had recently shut down Public Beta and was searching for the next chapter in his entrepreneurial journey while struggling to find a work-life balance. Adii's honesty and humility really shine through in the episode, and it was the first time I felt like we'd really captured something special.

One of my favorite stories he told us was about how he'd recently caught himself getting wrapped up in raising funding, simply because he could. He had a vague business idea, but because of his previous success with WooThemes, he found it easy to raise millions for his next venture. The thing was, he wasn't quite ready to run that fast, and he realized it. So he told us, **"Simplify things. Go back to basics. Create something of value that someone else wants to pay you for."** That has become his mantra ever since.

The biggest lesson for me from Adii was a personal one. Adii talked about his quest to find work-life balance after being heavily focused on WooThemes for so long. **"The biggest thing in finding balance is to obey the physical signs your mind and your body impose on you."** I remember wanting to give him a big hug after he said this. I had been working hard to build a self-sustaining product company. It had been five years since I'd taken a proper vacation, and I typically ended up working through weekends, holidays, and most every other life event. As an entrepreneur, this is what you do sometimes, but I'd been ignoring those physical signs, and it was time to stop. So I began going to the gym regularly, eating better, stopped drinking beer, and cutting back on caffeine. After a couple of months, it started to have an amazing effect on my overall happiness. What really drove the lesson home for me was seeing how much overlap there was between our struggles at the time.

The big lesson from our chat came when he talked about launching Public Beta with little more than a landing page. **"Without a product, in a week or two, I captured $4,000 in revenue. That adds a lot of momentum to an idea."** He describes wanting to not only validate the idea but to make sure it was something people wanted to pay for. How did he do this? Simply by requiring a credit card up front and using content to drive traffic to the landing page. He didn't tell people he didn't have anything to sell yet (which did end up getting some backlash) as that wouldn't have been a true test of whether or not people were willing to buy it.

What was the big advantage of doing this over traditional customer development? Adii breaks it down into two major advantages:

1. Having cash on hand, up front, to help build your initial version
2. Being able to learn from actual customers with a vested interest in the company

When people put down money for a solution, it made a big difference in the conversations he had with them. Instead of discussing what they were willing to pay for, he was able to get to what they needed in order to feel they were getting value from the product.

While your execution of this technique may differ, getting to the root of how people actually feel about your solution and getting honest feedback from your customers or potential customers is an important aspect of early product development.

Entrepreneurial life is hard, but make sure you take care of yourself because this isn't a sprint, it's a marathon. Taking a deep breathe and making sure that you're putting your time and energy into a validated idea can make all the difference.

"IF THEY'RE NOT RESONATING WITH THE PROBLEM, THEY'RE **NEVER** GOING TO CARE ABOUT YOUR SOLUTION."

Mikael Cho
FOUNDER CREW

"THE KEY IS YOU HAVE TO JUST START."

Nick O'Neill
CEO HOLLER

"I DON'T HAVE A SUCCESS METRIC…IT'S REALLY THE
HUMAN CONNECTION THAT BLOGGING CAN ENABLE
THAT MAKES IT SUPER VALUABLE TO ME."

Ryan Hoover
FOUNDER PRODUCT HUNT

"MOST THINGS DON'T WORK THE FIRST TIME YOU TRY, OR EVEN THE SECOND TIME. KEEP TWEAKING."

Sean Ellis
CEO QUALAROO

"ALWAYS BE BUILDING YOUR PEOPLE PIPELINE."

Melanie Gordon
CEO TAPHUNTER

"Don't be afraid to ask people to put down their email. Don't be afraid to ask people to pay money."

Chris Hexton
CO-FOUNDER VERO

Ryan Carson

Episode 77

by Joelle Steiniger

Ryan Carson was a particularly special episode for me. His online school, Treehouse, literally changed my life.

When I learned to code through Treehouse courses two years ago, it unlocked the door to entrepreneurship for me. I'll never look back, and I have Ryan to thank for the skills that allow me to live my dream every day. Finally getting to speak with the man behind it all made it all the more rewarding when I realized how passionately and genuinely he cares about what he's doing and the people whose lives he's affecting.

"Before Treehouse, I thought: This isn't what I want to die doing. I want to die doing something bigger…. Now, we can actually affect someone's life. I'm so excited to be doing this. I don't have any intention of selling Treehouse. Ever."

He's hell-bent on a mission to change the world and the lives of people who can now (unlike just a few years ago) become job-ready, without debt, in a matter of months. **"I'm so lucky to be doing something that I enjoy. A lot of people don't have the opportunity to pick their career or to have skills that are needed."** As he aims to change that, he also brings his mission inward by empowering his own employees to have ownership over their careers.

Ryan doesn't do much by the book. He built Treehouse as a distributed team working only four days a week. On top of that, they recently transitioned the company to a flat structure, eliminating all managers and layers of the organization. It changed everything. **"As soon as people have power to choose what they do, their happiness level goes up exponentially. It's incredibly empowering."** Every member of the team can propose projects to work on, ways to measure success, and resources needed. If other people on the team like the idea and see value, they join the project and do the work. Later, teammates anonymously review each other and everyone is held accountable for their work.

Rather than following a traditional structure of top-down management, which Ryan describes as being **"designed for unhappiness — to empower few people and dis-empower everyone else,"** he's ignored convention and empowered the many. With a team behind him that has helped Treehouse hit profitability only a few years after raising $13 million, enroll almost 100,000 students all over the world, and become one of the most desired companies to work for, I think it's safe to say it's working.

In the tech industry especially, people love to talk about disruption: about doing things differently, changing the world, setting new precedents. Rarely is it actually the case that they're doing it instead of just talking about it. With Ryan, I can whole-heartedly say it's authentic through and through. He's written, **"There's no guarantee we'll succeed, but I'm going to die trying."** After talking with him, I don't have an ounce of doubt that he means it.

"It's important to have vision, but don't cling so tightly to it that you ignore what people say."

Drew Strojny
FOUNDER OF THE THEME FOUNDRY AND MEMBERFUL

"YOU CAN'T ALWAYS MAKE BUSINESS SCIENTIFIC,
YOU HAVE TO TRUST YOUR GUT."

Allan Branch
CO-FOUNDER LESS ACCOUNTING

"My advice to any early-stage company is to try a bunch of stuff and make sure you're measuring and testing."

Ben Sardella
CO-FOUNDER DATANYZE

"Networking is the content marketing secret that no one wants to talk about."

Gregory Ciotti
LEAD CONTENT STRATEGY HELP SCOUT

"You get to design the kind of company you work for. Culture has to be intentional."

Jesse Mecham
FOUNDER YOU NEED A BUDGET

"INVESTING IS LIKE BUYING HOMES. YOU NEED TO
BE CONSCIOUS OF WHAT'S ON THE MARKET AND
WHAT THEY'RE TRADING AT."

Elliot Schneier
COO FUNDABLE

Christine Lu

Episode 42

by Michael Sacca

I first met Christine after posting a story about depression in my family and how it's affected me in my entrepreneurial ventures. She's been a long time advocate for opening the conversation surrounding founder depression and has been incredibly open about sharing her own story. She's someone I genuinely look up to and have a deep respect for because of her courage to share openly on this topic.

When we recorded this, I was actually at a low point myself. I was stuck in a company that I'd built but no longer felt a part of. I'd burned through most of my savings trying to keep everything afloat; no matter what we tried, we couldn't hit the numbers we needed to, and everything seemed to be crumbling. It was not only defeating but incredibly stressful trying to "keep the lights on" while keeping a roof over my family's head.

As Christine points out, the major problem that surrounds mental health in the business world is the stigma. Most founders are Type A, highly-driven, overachieving, public figures and are under an immense amount of pressure from themselves, their company, and their community. Typically, founders feel they need to build an emotional wall in order to keep everything moving forward. Christine points out, though, **"If you can't talk to your co-founder or significant other, something's wrong."** This is not to say that you shouldn't do your best to keep a strong face for your company and your investors, but having someone to have those real conversations with from time to time is an essential tool for founders.

What I loved about talking to Christine was her genuine concern for people, especially in the startup community. She pointed out that more and more incubators and accelerators were starting, and **"nobody wants to fail, but 90% of us will."** What happens to those founders who do? We lack an infrastructure as a community to give the proper support to those who need it, and yet we're encouraging more and more people to take this path. There's an imbalance there, but we can help fix it by sharing our stories and connecting with people, as people.

One of the biggest insights I got from Christine was simply about being open and honest. It's something that's incredibly hard to do, as it's always scary to share what's really going on when it's not going well. The thing is, it can help break down the barriers of what's happening with you, and even help someone else in need. When you open up, it gives others a chance to share their story with you, increases peoples awareness of what you're experiencing, and allows you an opportunity to connect with people who may be able to help. It creates healing. When we break down stigmas, especially relating to mental health, we're able to connect with each other on a deeper level and help others (and ourselves) before it's too late.

I'll leave you with my favorite quote from Christines Twitter stream: **"Hope you all have someone you can be real with when not sharing selfies of you 'killin it'."**

I honestly hope you do.

"I REFUSE TO BELIEVE THAT YOU'VE GOT TO LOSE DOUBLE DIGIT MILLIONS TO BUILD A BIG BUSINESS."

Nick Francis
CO-FOUNDER HELPSCOUT

"ANALYTICS IS ABOUT LISTENING TO WHY THINGS HAPPENED, NOT JUST WHAT HAPPENED."

Lee Jacobson
CEO APMETRIX

"We all have the same ideas - it comes down to execution."

Pieter Levels
FOUNDER LEVELS.IO

"HAVING LIVE CHAT IN YOUR ONBOARDING CAN BE
A REAL CANARY IN A COAL MINE."

Samuel Hulick
FOUNDER USERONBOARD.COM

"FUNDRAISING GUARANTEES NOTHING ABOUT
YOUR ULTIMATE SUCCESS."

Alex Moore
CEO BAYDIN

"The one thing I recommend everyone think about is: Are you working on the right thing, right now?"

Hiten Shah
CO-FOUNDER KISSMETRICS & CRAZYEGG

A LOOK INSIDE

Jason Cohen
Episode 27

by Matt Goldman

Our chat with Jason Cohen was one of the few talks that stopped me in my tracks and encouraged me to rethink everything about entrepreneurship.

In the short span of about 45 minutes, he helped us to basically understand that all anyone is doing in the startup world is making deals — just like any other industry. Not all deals are alike, despite what you read on sites like Hacker News and in the countless blog posts out there about funding, growth, product development, and so on.

He taught us that, at the end of the day, you need to look at what you want out of your company, be deliberate, and do what you've got to do to achieve those goals.

What did that look like for Jason? This is how he described himself during the intro: **"WP Engine is my 4th startup. I've done bootstrapped startups; I've raised money, as a co-founder, as a single founder, in hardware and in software. Two of the companies have sold, and all of the companies made more than a million in annual revenue while I was running them. I'm the CTO and founder of WP Engine and today, we have about 140 employees and we're growing fast. This is one of those raise money and grow fast sort of companies. Even though I'm currently in a company in which we decided to raise money, I'm also extremely partial to bootstrapped companies as well. I think they don't get a fair shake in the world, especially in the online tech world, where if you're not valued at a billion dollars regardless of revenue, then you're nothing."**

Talking with someone who's seen so many aspects of this industry, and who wasn't afraid to have an unpopular opinion, was so valuable!

Also, Jason shook up my beliefs around startup fundraising. At the time, I had been searching for companies that weren't bootstrapped but that also weren't seeking large VC rounds of funding. I wanted to talk to the entrepreneurs who had raised some money from angel investors to get an accelerated start, but who also intended on becoming profitable before needing further investment.

First, he taught us that regardless of whether or not you'll be raising funding, it's best to hit profitability as soon as possible for the sake of leverage.

"The best position to be in is one in which you don't need the money — so you can walk away."

With WP Engine, they hit profitability twice in their first 18 months, and they then began to see the benefits of raising money and "going big" with their idea. The conditions of their product and market made it a very sensible decision.

Also, Jason's opinion regarding finding that funding "middle ground" surprised me: **"Profitability is the last thing you want — it indicates that you're out of ideas of how to grow."**

Since talking to Jason, we've seen over a hundred creative ways to raise funding, seek profitability, ignore profitability, hire fast, hire slow, and so on — and it only reinforced what we began to learn with Jason: There is no right or wrong route; just the appropriate route for you and your company.

"These goals are not right or wrong. What is wrong is when you have something that would make you happy, but instead you do behaviors or actions that are along a different goal. Or if you don't decide the goal, and so you sort of do a little bit of everything, and therefore nothing particularly well — those are wrong choices."

"FISH WHERE THE FISH ARE."

Leslie Bradshaw
MANAGING PARTNER MADEBYMANY

"You're not the hero of your startup's story; *YOUR CUSTOMER IS*."

Josh Anon
CEO VISIONEER STUDIOS

"THERE'S AN ENORMOUS AMOUNT OF TENSION, SUCCESS, FAILURE, AND BETRAYAL THAT HAPPENS IN THE VENTURE WORLD."

Eliot Peper
AUTHOR UNCOMMON STOCK

"If you can't talk to your co-founder or significant other, something's wrong."

Christine Lu
CEO AFFINITY CHINA

"THE KEY DIFFERENCE BETWEEN CUSTOMER DEVELOPMENT AND WORKING ON TRACTION IS GOING THROUGH MARKETING CHANNELS."

Gabriel Weinberg
FOUNDER DUCKDUCKGO & AUTHOR TRACTION

"People don't connect with what you built or how you built it. They connect with why you built it."

Jeremiah Gardner
AUTHOR THE LEAN BRAND

A LOOK INSIDE
Perri Blake Gorman
Episode 21

by Joelle Steiniger

Perri Blake Gorman was our first female guest on the podcast. I was naturally very excited to talk to her not only for that reason, but because she's also a non-technical founder. What I wasn't expecting was how inspired I would be by her story, her outlook on life, and her principles for building a business.

"I don't wait until I need something to create relationships with people. I do it as a practice." Perri has turned relationship building into an art form. And the reason she's so good at it is because she genuinely cares about people. It's authentic. It's part of who she is, it's why she was a great recruiter, and it's why she's been able to build a product around the needs of people who also care about people. We all may not be able to focus as much on relationship building as Perri (it is her job, after all), but consider this: **"If you only talk to people when you need them, that's what they'll associate your calls with. As opposed to the other way around."** Is that really how you want others to view you?

Her outlook on entrepreneurship really stuck with me as well. **"When you look at founders who continue to survive, they're the ones who find the magic door through the brick wall."** What she's talking about is the ability to believe that you'll find success. We all have self-doubt. But the entrepreneurs who always seem to be around in the long-haul are the ones that believe they can make it work. They find the "magic door" to get through every brick wall that gets in their way. Not through brute force -- but by being open to ideas and solutions, knowing that there is a way to move ahead. This mindset is so incredibly powerful, especially for young entrepreneurs like us with long, uncertain futures ahead.

When we recorded this episode, she was about 18 months into her venture working on Archively. When I asked what she'd do differently if she could go back, her answer really struck me: **"Nothing,"** she said. **"I believe you have to have gone through all the things you went through to get to where you are now."** We love to look back and recount all the things we'd change for the better. We imagine a scenario in which we use our newfound knowledge to get from A to B faster, avoid all mistakes, do everything right the first time, and all live happily ever after. But the truth is, we undervalue where that knowledge came from. Those mistakes, those dead-ends, they were vastly more valuable than the times we got it right the first time. It's not fun. Failure sucks. But a different perspective, an appreciation for the path that got us to where we are now and where we'll be next, makes everything so much more fulfilling.

I guess what I loved most about this episode is that all of these lessons apply just as much to life as they do business. So, no matter what business you're in or what you choose to do with your life, take a lesson from Perri and do the following: build genuine relationships, believe you'll make it through any brick wall, and enjoy the journey.

"THE GOAL WITH ANY CONTENT IS TO CREATE SOMETHING THAT MOVES YOUR AUDIENCE EMOTIONALLY."

Mark Fidelman

CEO OF RAYNFOREST, FORBES COLUMNIST, AND AUTHOR SOCIALIZED!

"It's not about *CAN* you build the product. The question is, *SHOULD* you build the product?"

Brant Cooper
AUTHOR THE LEAN ENTREPRENEUR

"Whenever you meet someone new, ask them one question. Answer ten."

Oli Gardner
CO-FOUNDER UNBOUNCE

"Simplify things. Go back to basics. Create something of value that someone else wants to pay you for."

———

Adii Pienaar
FOUNDER WOOTHEMES AND RECEIPTFUL

"Focus on doing just a few things. Do them really, really good. Then focus on the next thing."

Mo Plassnig
CEO CODESHIP

"SOLVE PROBLEMS WHERE PEOPLE ARE ALREADY PAYING FOR SOLUTIONS."

Dan Norris
CO-FOUNDER OF WPCURVE, BLACK HOPS BEER AND HELLOIFY

Conrad Egusa

Episode 41

by Joelle Steiniger

When we interviewed Conrad about public relations for startups, I was expecting to run through a string of tactics and tricks for "hacking your way" onto the front page of TechCrunch. We tech folks can be short-sighted like that sometimes. We're so used to the ease of dumping messaging out through our social media channels and finding hacks and shortcuts to get noticed, that we overlook the importance of strategy and the fundamentals of traditional PR, which are as impactful and effective as ever.

While we did walk away with an arsenal of techniques to execute on, I took something much deeper away from our chat with Conrad: **"Sell the why, not the what."** In other words, what's your story? What's your angle? Why should anyone care about what you're doing? We've become completely numb to funding announcements like "TechCo Raises $10 Million Dollars A Round". But that's not really the story they're aiming to tell. They're trying to convey that someone has a big vision for something, and other people believe so strongly in it that they're willing to put a lot of money behind it.

Most of us aren't raising giant rounds worthy of writing about. So what's our story? Why are we relevant? Conrad gave the example of the coworking space, Espacio, he founded in Medellín, Colombia. When he reached out to TechCrunch and others, he didn't approach them with the angle, "We're opening a co-working space with 40 desks, fully stocked kitchen, etc." That's not interesting. What is interesting is, **"We're opening this coworking space to turn Medellín into the Silicon Valley of South America."** That's a story. It doesn't matter that he hasn't succeeded yet. His mission, his why, is compelling.

Considering this, it made me think much more deeply about my own story with HookFeed. It may do 20 things, but what does it really do? Or rather, what does it allow you to do? What's the single thing about it that's amazing, better, disruptive?

Why did we even build it, and who for? Thinking like this, especially for the sake of messaging, actually re-introduced me to Jobs-to-Be-Done exercises and changed the way I approach talking about, writing about, and thinking about HookFeed. And, it set me up for success on his next piece of advice.

"Reduce the friction it takes a journalist to write your article." Most journalists are paid per article. Beyond considering if it's a story worth writing (if you followed the advice above, it should be), they'll consider how much effort it will take to write. Conrad's advice: **"Reverse-engineer the article you want them to write into a press release."** Don't just deliver a boilerplate "announcement;" give them some fuel. Tell them what's interesting or unique about you as a founder. Dig up supporting data points to further your relevance (e.g., market size, market trends, number of users) Put yourself in their shoes and think about the kind of information they might have to gather to bring context to the story. Then deliver it to them. Not only will you have more control framing your story the way you want to tell it, but you'll greatly increase your chances of getting it published. This piece of advice actually applies to most favors you ask of people. If you want someone to do something for you, make it as easy as possible for them to do it!

If you haven't done so in a while, I encourage you to spend some time thinking about your story. Go through the exercise of writing a press release (even if it's going to end up in the trash). And when you do so, ask yourself: What is your overarching vision, or mission for your company, and why is it relevant?

"THE BEST THING YOU CAN DO IS TO MAKE IT AS EASY AS POSSIBLE FOR SOMEONE ELSE TO PROMOTE YOU."

Ruben Gamez
FOUNDER BIDSKETCH

"Don't spend time optimizing for an outcome that won't come. Your main goal is to build your business."

Brad Flora
CEO PERFECT AUDIENCE

"More features does not equal
technological progress.
Taking things away does."

David Warren
CEO LIA

"WORKING MORE THAN 40 HOURS A WEEK CONSISTENTLY JUST ISN'T A SUSTAINABLE WAY TO GO THROUGH LIFE."

Garrett Dimon
FOUNDER SIFTER AND AUTHOR OF STARTING + SUSTAINING

"FIND A NICHE AND TACKLE IT."

Janine Sickmeyer
CEO NEXTCHAPTER

"IF YOU WEREN'T GETTING PAID TOMORROW,
WHAT WOULD YOU DO?"

Rob Mallery
VP OF TALENT ORIGINATE

Allan has a diverse background, from running a consultancy to hosting conferences to running their SaaS product, Less Accounting.

And it was clear in talking with Allan that he has learned so much over the years as he's struggled to find his sweet spot. What's most admirable about the way he works is that he's realized he wants to be in this business for the long haul and therefore needs to find a way to make it sustainable.

He has set out to limit his hours spent working so that he can spend more time with his family and to create the perfect job that he'd be ecstatic doing for the next 20-30 years. And he's not just writing a Medium post about it; he's actually doing it.

He and his partner, Steve, work about 35 hours per week, take one week off from work every month, and Allan goes into work early so that he can feel good about leaving in the early afternoon to hang out with his kids.

"Whatever I don't get done [in my 35 hours] is not important."

Hearing him talk about his work was super refreshing because it's clear that he's come to realize that hours spent doesn't necessarily equate to progress.

"Everything can wait -- nothing's really that important."

He knows that he can wait to open that email, or that he could probably just delete it, and everything would be fine. If it's really important, the person will follow up. He also uses followup.cc, and I use Mailbox, to accomplish the reverse -- deferring emails until later.

Accepting that emails and other distractions can wait is so freeing. Accepting that you can say no to requests or defer them for months is downright liberating. It makes it possible for Allan to say things like, **"Yesterday, I was like 'Fuck this…. I'm going sailing.'"** Because he wanted to go sailing with his kids, and he valued that experience over whatever he was going to accomplish at work that day.

More people should strive to be like Allan, putting experiences ahead of their startups, and realizing the value of the time spent with friends and family. Allan has done what the smartest small business owners have done in the past: removed themselves partially from their business.

Allan knows that if the servers crash while he is away, his team can handle the problem without calling him. He's made the decision, and done what needed to be done, to unlock the lifestyle he wanted.

On the business side of things, he wanted to ensure that he'd be pumped about working on Less Accounting for many years to come since they have no plans of selling, so he designed the perfect job. He loves working on projects as inspiration strikes, and being creative in general, so he's modifying his content marketing strategy to jive with that. He knows he'll burn out if he has to write content about accounting/bookkeeping tricks for 20 years. He wants the freedom to be able to write about fun projects they're working on or non-tech endeavors, like setting up a distillery. Most would think that wouldn't be possible. But look at a company like MailChimp -- it's all in the branding.

You can create the perfect company for yourself. The kind of company you (and your team) will love for years to come.

"Don't just do what everyone else is doing - do what gives you a competitive advantage."

Rob Meadows
CEO ORIGINATE

"IF YOU ONLY TALK TO PEOPLE WHEN YOU NEED
THEM, THAT'S ALL THEY'LL ASSOCIATE
YOUR CALLS WITH."

Perri Blake Gorman
FOUNDER ARCHIVELY

"You need to say no to some things and yes to the things you want to be doing 6 months from now."

Steve P. Young
HOST MOBILE APP CHAT

"WE BOOTSTRAPPED BEFORE THE TERM EXISTED, AND FROM THE START SAID *WE'RE GOING TO CHARGE FOR THIS*"

Rob Mueller
CO-FOUNDER FASTMAIL

"You may think you're up against Goliath, but it's really much more of a level playing field than you think."

Todd Garland
FOUNDER BUYSELLADS

Rocketship.fm

www.ingramcontent.com/pod-product-compliance
Lightning Source LLC
Chambersburg PA
CBHW041453210326
41599CB00005B/240